Kittens'

DAY BOOK

With dearest love to my daughters
Virginia and Fiona

1998, Published by Rebo Productions Ltd.

Design and Created by Consortium, England
Written and compiled by Joan Moore
Photographs by Marc Henrie

D0259UK

Printed in Slovenia
ISBN 1 84053 056 1

Kittens'

DAY BOOK

January

The **January** kitten can be extrovert, rebellious and highly unpredictable. It is also a more than average intelligent puss. On its good behaviour, this little soul is loyal to its owner and charming in company. When it's naughty, this kitten can be stubborn, erratic and very single-minded. Looking neat and trim in kittenhood, the January kitten will grow into a smart, elegant-looking cat with an autocratic air and long, slender legs. Its wild elfin look is emphasised by widely spaced eyes and pointed ears. Preferring to watch TV or video, this cool kitten wouldn't be caught dead catching mundane mice!

January

Top Cat
On September 6, 1950, a four month-old kitten belonging to Josephine Aufdenblatten of Geneva, Switzerland was said to have followed a group of climbers to the top of the 4,478 metre Matterhorn in the Alps. An impossible feat? Perhaps the answer is that its owner lived quite near the summit!

~ 1 ~

~ 2 ~

~ 3 ~

~ 4 ~

Kitten Names
January kittens are independent, intelligent, unpredictable, cool and 'airy'. Names for your **January** boy kitten could be: Ariel, Seagull, Comet, CoolMcCool, Macintosh, Jack Frost, Prince Crispin, Peregrine, Lightning, Einstein; and for your **January** girl kitten: Snow Princess, Celeste, Little Snowdrop, Christobel, Diamond Ice, Bluebird, Azureyes, Aquamarina, Silvie, Diamante or Selina.

~ 5 ~

~ 6 ~

~ 7 ~

January

Kittens love to climb into things, and these four little ones make a very pretty picture sitting in their basket. But young kittens don't sit still for long; in seconds, they will be running around and getting into lots of mischief!

January

~ 8 ~

~ 9 ~

'Alexander preferred dairy foods to meat. Perhaps that accounted for his pale, creamy coat and gentle delicacy of nature. He was particularly fond of soft, cumbly cheese – he'd sniff around it, paw it gently and then consume it with great relish – to the disgust of his siblings!'

JOAN MOORE

~ 10 ~

~ 11 ~

KITTEN CARE
When buying a pedigree kitten, choose the one which is lively and active with clean eyes and ears and no sign of soiling beneath the tail. The kitten should be at least twelve weeks old before leaving its mother. Remember to collect the following items from the breeder: your kitten's pedigree, registration and inoculation certificates, a suitable diet sheet and, if possible, a list of do's and don'ts on rearing your chosen breed of kitten. Introduce your new kitten to your vet as soon as possible after you acquire it. The chances are that they will soon become good friends!

~ 12 ~

~ 13 ~

~ 14 ~

January

~ 15 ~

~ 16 ~

~ 17 ~

Intoxicated Kits
Don't be surprised if the cat-nip mouse you buy for your kitten to play with sends it into ecstasies! Cat nip *(Nepata cataria)* produces a scent which is most intoxicating to the feline kind, and they often fall into a trance-like state which can last for ten minutes or more.

~ 18 ~

~ 19 ~

~ 20 ~

~ 21 ~

January

Friendly Felines
Kittens make great friends and comforters. Theophile Gautier wrote: 'He makes himself the companion of your hours of solitude, melancholy and toil. He remains for whole evenings on your knee, uttering his contented purr, happy to be with you and forsaking the company of others of his own species.'

~ 22 ~

~ 23 ~

~ 24 ~

~ 25 ~

~ 26 ~

Kitten Care
You will need to acquire the following basic equipment *before* you say 'welcome home' to your new kitten. These are: a medium size, draught-proof cardboard box or basket, lined with a small warm blanket; non-spill food and water dishes and appropriate kitten food. Cuddly toys and cat-nip mice come later!

~ 27 ~

~ 28 ~

January

~ 29 ~

~ 30 ~

~ 31 ~

Choosing your kitten

Whether you choose a pedigree or a non-pedigree kitten – and rescued kittens are also in this last category – you'll find that they're all delightfully different; each with their individual personality traits and characteristics. Kittens come in various coat patterns: tabby, tortoiseshell, agouti, tri- and bi-colour and self. All of these can be seen in many different colours and coat lengths: longhair, semi-longhair or shorthair. It is great fun to watch your kitten grow into a fine, healthy cat. Give it lots of love and tender care and it will reward you with loyalty and affection for a long time to come.

February

The **February** kitten is a dreamer and sits quietly on a warm windowsill far away in its own little fantasy world. This small creature is gentle, intuitive and can create a rare spiritual bond with its owner, bringing inspiration, insight and compassion to the relationship. The February kitten is soft and fluffy with gentle little paws – keeping its claws hidden so that only *very* rarely will you receive a painful scratch. With a kind, gentle heart, all small furry toys are its very best friends, and it will cuddle up tight keeping them – and itself – as warm as toast.

February

~ 1 ~

~ 2 ~

TWO'S COMPANY

Kittens are cute and cuddly, and great fun to watch and play with, but they are also demanding on your time and attention. A kitten by itself is playful and inquisitive and will get into all kinds of mischief! So, when you buy your first kitten, why not get two? They will be company for each other and will play together quite happily, perhaps not keeping out of mischief altogether, but they'll be good companions as they grow into adulthood. And who knows? They may enjoy great times, chatting to each other and sharing their happy memories as kittens together!

~ 3 ~

~ 4 ~

~ 5 ~

~ 6 ~

~ 7 ~

February

Kittens, like cats, can sleep lightly or 'catnap' frequently and for short periods of time. Young kittens are full of energy, play with great enthusiasm and can go from playing to sleeping in the wink of an eye. Overall, they can sleep as much as 20 hours in each 24!

February

~ 8 ~

~ 9 ~

'Scraps was the smallest kitten. He loved to have his ears washed, and the sight of him sitting tall, his tiny oval feet pressed close together and small seal face with eyes shut tight straining up to his mother's rough tongue was one I shall always remember.'

JOAN MOORE

~ 10 ~

~ 11 ~

~ 12 ~

~ 13 ~

~ 14 ~

CLEAN KITTIES

Kittens need to be trained to use a litter tray and this the mother cat can do most effectively. When the kittens are first born, their mother stimulates their eliminatory processes by licking the kitten under the tail. When the kitten reaches two or three weeks old, it is using a corner of the nesting box for this purpose. At around three to four weeks old the mother will have carried them to the litter tray and have taught the kittens to use it properly. This early training effectively ensures the kitten's 'clean habits' for the rest of its life.

February

"These books smell interesting!" Cats and kittens are renowned for their love of books – they can't wait for their owner to settle down for a quiet read before they are sitting on the open book 'pawing' over every word.

February

~ 15 ~

~ 16 ~

Kitten Names

February kittens are gentle, dreamy, intuitive, psychic and 'watery'. Names for your **February** boy kitten could be: Kipper, Skipper, Neptune, Jupiter, Davy Jones, Marmaduke, Valentino, Dab'n'Flounder, Horatio Nelson, Moonlight Mariner, Kingfisher; and for your **February** girl kitten: Pussy Willow, Columbine, Nereid, Rainbow, Iris, Angelica, Roxanne, Princess, Our Secret or Elvira.

~ 17 ~

~ 18 ~

~ 19 ~

~ 20 ~

~ 21 ~

February

Kittens like to explore the great outdoors – especially the adventurous Abyssinian breed. These dainty ones are being very brave. They've discovered an exciting wilderness – a forest of green leaves and sweet-smelling earth, right at the bottom of their garden!

February

~ 22 ~

EARLY LEARNING
Kittens can be gentle or fierce. From an early age, kittens are learning and preparing themselves for life as a hunter when they reach adulthood. One piece of learning behaviour is play-fighting, and if your kitten demonstrates this forcibly on your hand, its teeth and claws can be very painful!

~ 23 ~

~ 24 ~

There's a knack in teaching young kittens to feed themselves. Begin by dipping the kits' mouths into a little milk and warm water. They will rather resent this treatment at first... the cunning ones will grasp the situation and make another attempt on their own account!'
FRANCES SIMPSON
(c1902)

~ 25 ~

~ 26 ~

~ 27 ~

~ 28-29 ~

February

As soon as they are born, mother cat washes each of her kittens thoroughly with her rough tongue. This clears away ambiotic fluids and other birthing material, to reveal a sparkling brand new kitten! She continues the washing routine until the kittens learn to lick their paws and wash themselves.

March

The **March** kitten is a dynamic bundle of fluff; self-willed and full of the joys of spring. A creature of impulse and remarkably fearless, this kitten leaps and bounds, and plays around with effortless grace -- like a leaf in a mad March wind. Its antics are a constant surprise, as are its wild, willful ways and mischievous grin. "Whatever will it do next?" you ask yourself. Kittens born in March are their own creatures and bear allegiance to no-one but themselves. With an intense fiery energy, the March kitten is first to the food bowl – and first into trouble!

March

~ 1 ~

~ 2 ~

~ 3 ~

A legend says that a litter of kittens was thrown into a river to drown. On its banks the mother cat cried bitterly and the willows growing by the riverside wondered how they could help the poor mother's kittens. They decided to spread out their long branches so that the kittens could easily reach them and so climb out of the river. Since that time, each year in the springtime the willows bear velvet-like buds which to the touch feel similar to the soft coat of a kitten. Recalling their former act of kindness, the trees are known as pussy-willows...

~ 4 ~

~ 5 ~

~ 6 ~

~ 7 ~

March

"If I keep very, very still, will they guess that I'm here? I'll just pretend that I'm an ornament and they'll never know!" Pussy cats on shelves? Oh no, that will never do! Come on down little puss, before you break something!

March

~ 8 ~

~ 9 ~

'There's a superstition that it is unlucky ever to weigh your kitten, but I think it's a useful way of finding out whether your puss keeps in good health. If I found my cat was rapidly getting lighter, I should give a course of cod liver oil...'
FRANCES SIMPSON (c 1902)

~ 10 ~

~ 11 ~

~ 12 ~

~ 13 ~

~ 14 ~

KITTEN CARE
During the first days of a kitten's life, its eyes and ears are closed. At a week old, the tiny ears are still folded and the eyes are just beginning to open. To avoid bright light causing the kitten distress, it's advisable to keep the nesting box in semi-darkness at this stage. The kitten's eyes are a bluish-grey for the first four or five weeks of its life, then their colour changes to varying shades of green, amber or gold. Certain pedigree breeds, such as the Siamese, have bright blue eyes; some odd-eyed breeds have one blue and one orange.

March

~ 15 ~

~ 16 ~

~ 17 ~

~ 18 ~

~ 19 ~

~ 20 ~

~ 21 ~

KITTEN NAMES

March kittens are fearless, impulsive, reckless and 'fiery'. Names for your **March** boy kitten could be: Fiery Jack, Ace, Captain, Ignatius, Tantivy, Redalert, Ginger, Apache, Geronimo, Chanticleer, Scaramouche, Speedy Gonzales, Sparky; and for your **March** girl kitten: Spitfire, Chillichilli, Miss Scarlett, Wanda, Zizkatz, Carmen Miranda, Coppernob, Topaz, Caprice or Esprit.

March

~ 22 ~

Record-breaker
The largest litter of kittens on record numbered 19! Four were stillborn, and all were born after a 70-day gestation period. The clever mum on this occasion was four year-old Burmese, Tarawood Antigone, from Oxfordshire in England. The 15 survivors, 14 of them male, all grew to be strong, healthy adults.

~ 23 ~

~ 24 ~

~ 25 ~

~ 26 ~

Kitten Care
Kittens like to be cosy and warm, and like snuggling up to mum's furry body. If the kitten is still with its littermates, piling on top of one another is another way of keeping warm. For the single kitten, a hot water-bottle protected by a towel or blanket is comforting.

~ 27 ~

~ 28 ~

March

~ 29 ~

~ 30 ~

~ 31 ~

"We're as good as gold; no trouble at all. That is, until we jump down and start to fight!" Three little Somali kittens – tiny jungle cats in long coats, as delectable as kittens can be but sometimes they're naughty too!

April

The **April** kitten is a steadfast little puss. It is languidly placid, preferring home comforts to exploring the delights of next door's garden. The pleasantly purring April puss is not the most active feline in the world, but between bouts of dreamless sleep it can be quite territorial and will defend its patch with passion and feeling! Appreciation of life's luxuries – like food – means keeping a keen eye on kitten's weight. 'A fit kitten is not a fat kitten' is the key phrase. However, this sturdy little creature can be very loving, and petting and pampering will bring rich rewards.

April

~ 1 ~

~ 2 ~

'It is an inconvenient habit of kittens (Alice had once remarked) that whatever you say to them, they always purr.'
Lewis Carroll *(Alice in Wonderland)*. Author Pam Brown also saw two sides to the kitten: 'Kittens are wide-eyed, soft and sweet. With needles in their jaws and feet.'

~ 3 ~

~ 4 ~

KITTEN NAMES
April kittens are patient, placid, purry, steadfast, possessive and 'earthy'. Names for your **April** boy kitten could be: Morpheus, Minos, Caruso, Purralot, Maverick, Nature Boy, Placido, Methusalah, Seth: and for your **April** girl kitten: Sabra, Avril, Dawn, Asphodel, Hugs'n'kisses, Maria Callas, Gypsy, Owlet, Placida, Purrypuss, Minah Bird or Princess Purrfect.

~ 5 ~

~ 6 ~

~ 7 ~

April

"What's this? I haven't seen anything like it before! I'll catch it before it flies away!" Kittens play for hours with dangling toys on pieces of string. But always supervise this game, to avoid accidents happening to your pet.

April

~ 8 ~

~ 9 ~

Ralph Waldo Emerson asks: 'Do you see that kitten chasing so prettily her own tail? If you could look with her eyes, you might see her surrounded with hundreds of figures performing complex dramas, with tragic and comic issues, long conversations, many characters, many ups and downs of fate.'

~ 10 ~

~ 11 ~

~ 12 ~

~ 13 ~

~ 14 ~

April

"Hello there! Can I see our dinner being prepared? Hey, wake up!" But Ginger's had a hard day playing games with his little brother. "I'm tired and I'd rather go to sleep." "OK, but can I have yours?"

April

Mother Care
After about three weeks, kittens start to walk around and explore their little world. Since they are beginning to get inquisitive about their environment, they often try to climb out of their nest. Mother cat will then rescue her kittens and bring them back. When she has lots of kittens in the litter, Mum is kept on the go and has to be very patient with her mischievous babies – sometimes letting them know who's boss! When carrying them back in her mouth to safety, Mum will grip her kitten by the fold of skin at the back of the neck.

Kitten Care
Be affectionate with your kitten. Hold it gently in your lap, cuddle it close to you on your shoulder and talk to it gently. Conversation is very important and soon your kitten will begin to understand and respond to your voice, and you will both be chatting away quite happily!

~ 15 ~

~ 16 ~

~ 17 ~

~ 18 ~

~ 19 ~

~ 20 ~

~ 21 ~

April

Kittens are so naturally inquisitive that they will often scale objects – such as steps – a lot larger or taller than themselves, just to satisfy that infamous curiosity which remains with them into adulthood.

April

~ 22 ~

By the time *Through the Looking Glass* and *What Alice Found There* were published in 1871, Alice's cat Dinah had two kittens, Kitten and Snowdrop. Portrayed by Lewis Carroll as the Red Queen and the White Queen, these two young kittens went through the magical 'Looking Glass' with Alice...

~ 23 ~

~ 24 ~

~ 25 ~

~ 26 ~

~ 27 ~

~ 28 ~

April

~ 29 ~

~ 30 ~

'Is it those large luminous eyes, so guileless, trusting and steadfast in their gaze which enchants us into maternal ways? So that we nurture and cherish our kitten, well into adulthood, until she becomes our child no longer, but more a dear and much-loved sister and friend...'

Joan Moore

May

The **May** kitten is inquisitive, intelligent and at the same time restless and energetic. The myth that May kittens are susceptible to the Devil's influence is not so far from the truth – except that May babies are so exquisitely charming you really wouldn't suspect it. Even at an early age May kittens are great conversationalists, adept at getting their own way with winning smiles and vivacious chatter. With quick-wittedness and sheer cunning, this winsome little winner works out how to raid the refrigerator at an early age – and how to use the telephone. Be warned, the May myth is true!

May

~ 1 ~

~ 2 ~

~ 3 ~

~ 4 ~

~ 5 ~

~ 6 ~

~ 7 ~

Mother Care

The mother cat will often ignore her owner's arrangements for a nesting box and will hide her newborn kittens in a dark little place of her own choice. This spot will be sheltered, dry and, above all, private. Once she has prepared the nest for her kittens she will impregnate the bedding with her own body smell in order to attract the kittens, back to their home when they eventually begin to wander. Kittens may be moved several times – especially if the mother cat senses they are in danger or simply to avoid them being touched or handled by humans.

May

‘Mother cats are among the most devoted of domestic animals; they would lay down their lives for their kittens. I’ve heard of mother cats travelling great distances to bring home kittens who, in some strange clairvoyant way, they knew were not in good human hands...’

Juliette de Bairacli Levy

May

~ 8 ~

~ 9 ~

Little Devils

Kittens born in May are said to belong to the Devil, are little mischief-makers and more trouble than all other kittens put together! Reputedly, they come into the world when the marriage of the divine God and Goddess takes place, so making their tiny souls more vulnerable to demonic influence.

~ 10 ~

~ 11 ~

~ 12 ~

~ 13 ~

~ 14 ~

Early Learning

As kittens grow, they gradually develop their new skills of hunting and playing. Some of this behaviour is instinctive, but much of it is gained through experience. Hunting techniques are learned by watching their mother, and attack and defence techniques are often practised by waging fierce battles with their siblings!

May

‘For very delicate kittens, raw meat should be passed through a mincing machine, or, if the animal is extremely weak and ill, then let it be gently rubbed through a sieve. Teach your kittens when young to lap water...It is a capital thing for all animals...’
FRANCES SIMPSON (c 1902)

~ 15 ~

~ 16 ~

~ 17 ~

~ 18 ~

~ 19 ~

~ 20 ~

~ 21 ~

KITTEN NAMES
Your **May** boy kitten could be: Dandy Dancer, Little Monkey, Oberon, Puck, Hermes, Jackbenimble; and for your **May** girl kitten: Queenie, Faerie, Daisymae, Queen Mab, Aurora, Sweet Kate, Titania, Morwenna, Kittikeepstill, Butterfly, Gadabout, Lady Linnet or Twinkle Toes.

May

Kitten Care
There are lots of expensive and attractive cat beds to be found in pet shops and stores. Perhaps your kitten may even enjoy sleeping in the one you've just bought. In any event, make sure it's positioned in a secluded, draughtproof place – because, ultimately, all your sleepy kitten needs is a warm, comfortable spot, and won't any small basket or box equipped with a warm clean blanket suffice? However, don't be too surprised to find your kitten has decided to sleep just about anywhere that it chooses to sleep. As the author and cat-lover Eleanor Farjeon discovered: 'Cats sleep anywhere...'

~ 22 ~

~ 23 ~

~ 24 ~

~ 25 ~

~ 26 ~

~ 27 ~

~ 28 ~

May

~ 29 ~

~ 30 ~

~ 31 ~

Siamese kittens are like small white mice at birth, and their coats stay white until they are four to six weeks old. Then their immature 'points' begin to show; first on the tips of their ears and the tail, then on their nose and finally on their paws. Gradually, as they get older their 'mask' gets darker and spreads upwards towards the ears. At eight months old, the Siamese points should be well in evidence. Siamese cats were first introduced to the West in the 1880s, from the Royal Palace of Siam or Thailand, as we know it today.

June

The **June** kitten is gentle and loving and has one of the nicest natures around. June kit 'mothers' toys, slippers, trainers, small furry creatures (alive or stuffed) plus all manner of items which this maternally-minded purrson imagines lacks a mum. This kind 'n' cuddly little cat has a nice fluffy coat which makes a natural 'nest' for its potential brood. Another June baby trick: it learns early how to bring in 'presents' and keepsakes – all manner of interesting things – and hoard them away in your wardrobe or under the bed. From Day One, June kittens are nature's nurturers and carers.

June

~ 1 ~

~ 2 ~

~ 3 ~

~ 4 ~

~ 5 ~

~ 6 ~

~ 7 ~

MOTHER CARE

The newborn kitten is a tiny damp creature who cannot retain its body heat for very long so, as each of her babies is born, the mother cat licks it vigorously with her rough tongue, and then snuggles it quickly into her furry coat to keep it cosy. Usually, young kittens find it difficult to keep their body temperature up to a satisfactory level. So, to keep warm they burrow into their bedding or pile up together with their littermates. If they're still cold, they burrow to the bottom of the heap. This way, each kitten gets to keep warm.

June

The Persian Longhair is one of today's most popular breeds of cat. But to maintain their picture postcard looks, daily grooming is necessary. This Red Persian kitten looks in excellent condition with its already magnificent coat, ruff and ear furnishings.

June

These lovely little Silver Somali kittens pose very prettily and angelically for the camera. They make the most delightful subject for any phtographer. But the moment the camera has been put away, off they'll scurry getting up to all sorts of mischief!

June

June

~ 8 ~

~ 9 ~

Kitten Names
June kittens are gentle, loving, caring, maternally 'moony', avid collectors and 'watery'. Names for your **June** boy kitten could be: Captain Moonlight, Moonshine, Beachcomber, Moonwalker, Dreamer, Cuddles, Beamer; and for your **June** girl kitten: Selene, Sibyl, Astarte, Moonbeam, Phoebe, Bridget, Junebaby, Sylvie, Starry Eyes, Myrtle, Blossom, Mrs Mumcat or Bagpuss.

~ 10 ~

~ 11 ~

~ 12 ~

A comforting cat-nap... William S Burroughs' kitten stirs, ensuring his master's presence at his side: 'Purring in his sleep, Fletch stretches out his little black paw to touch my hands, the claws withdrawn, just a gentle touch to assure him that I am there beside him as he sleeps.'

~ 13 ~

~ 14 ~

June

~ 15 ~

~ 16 ~

~ 17 ~

~ 18 ~

~ 19 ~

~ 20 ~

~ 21 ~

Kitten Care
Everyone admires a sleek, well-groomed cat and from an early stage the grooming routine should form an essential part of a kitten's life. When your kitten is around six weeks old, gentle hand-grooming for five minutes or so will accustom it to this daily – and necessary – regime, and so prepare it for more serious grooming later on in adulthood. Special grooming equipment could include a soft brush, a wide-toothed comb and a grooming mitt, specially devised for grooming the shorthaired cat. For an extra glossy coat, use a chamois leather. Remember, you can't start a gentle grooming routine too early!

June

~ 22 ~

~ 23 ~

~ 24 ~

Early Training
A kitten is comparatively easy to train into good habits. While it's impossible to *force* a kitten to do anything, it *is* possible to encourage or discourage its actions. This takes a lot of patience and much gentle persuasion, but this way, training periods can be easy and even enjoyable.

~ 25 ~

~ 26 ~

Kitten Care
Carrying a kitten in your arms is difficult and can be dangerous. If frightened or curious, a kitten can suddenly leap, causing accidents to itself or others. The safest and easiest method of transportation, for instance when journeying to a cattery or the vet, is in a special carrying basket.

~ 27 ~

~ 28 ~

June

~ 29 ~

~ 30 ~

A snuggly bed is a favourite place for kittens. These two red and white ones look bright-eyed and lively but, as kittens do, they will soon fall asleep curled up cosily with each other, lost in the land of dreams...

July

The **July** kitten is 'larger than life'; it is regal and flamboyant in appearance and manner and destined to be a future 'king of the beasts'. Like the life-giving Sun, this kitten is glorious, stout-hearted, strong and we feel revitalized by its generous affections. Sincere and enthusiastic in its loyalty, it does, however, expect a 'lion's share' of devotion and can be pretty imperious if this is not forthcoming on demand. Eventually growing up to be a proud, protective parent, life is so much more rich and rewarding with a July kitten – they make all our days sunny ones.

July

~ 1 ~

~ 2 ~

'All kittens love fresh butter but, being rich and indigestible, it should be fed only in small amounts. The amount necessary to butter a new kitten's paws is permissible. Milk is a restorer in illness; especially when diluted with barley water and fortified with honey...'
JULIETTE DE BAIRACLI LEVY

~ 3 ~

~ 4 ~

~ 5 ~

KITTEN NAMES
July kittens are glorious, 'larger than life' limelight lovers, and 'fiery'. Names for your **July** boy kitten could be: Julius, Nero, Oscar, Zeus, Lionel, Aslan, Sovereign, Big Boy, Leo, Main Man, Sonny; and for your **July** girl kitten: Regina, Sunshine, Yurastar, Elsa, Juliana, Sarah Bernhardt, Big Bertha or Ethel Merman.

~ 6 ~

~ 7 ~

July

This British Shorthair Silver Tabby may look relaxed, but she's on alert where her kittens are concerned. What will they do next? But a sensible Mum cat knows that while they're playing, kittens are also learning – essential for healthy development.

July

~ 8 ~

Early Learning
Small kittens love the simplest of toys. For instance, a tightly rolled-up ball of paper will keep a playful kitten amused – and busy – for a long time! At least until it falls fast asleep in an exhausted little heap! Playtime for a kitten is a useful educative process; they practise their hunting skills, enabling basic feline instincts, such as chasing, pouncing and playing with prey, to develop. Mum will sometimes join in, too, swishing her tail from side to side so that the kittens can pounce on it and pretend that they're conquering a fierce animal out in the wild!

~ 9 ~

~ 10 ~

~ 11 ~

~ 12 ~

~ 13 ~

~ 14 ~

July

~ 15 ~

~ 16 ~

~ 17 ~

~ 18 ~

~ 19 ~

~ 20 ~

~ 21 ~

Record-breaker
The largest known litter in which all the kittens born survived belonged to Persian Longhair, Bluebell, who produced 14 healthy kittens in Wellington, Cape Province, South Africa in 1974. Black and white Tish from Yorkshire in England was 25 years old when she produced her 101st kitten in 1958.

Kitten Care
Keep a bowl of clean water available at all times. The feline digestive system sometimes cannot tolerate cows' milk, so offer it but *never* straight from the refrigerator, only if your kitten accepts it. Milky foods, like rice pudding or custard, are alternatives if your kitten cannot take raw milk.

July

~ 22 ~

~ 23 ~

~ 24 ~

Kitten Care
Cocksfoot grass is a healthy addition to your kitten's diet. As an optional extra, grass helps maintain a necessary balance to the digestive system. Cats in the wild with ready access to grass do this naturally, so why not offer your kitten grass in a pot, as an occasional nibble?

Cats tend not to make a fuss when they are unwell. Rather than seek sympathy, they prefer to retreat to a quiet corner and suffer in silence. Therefore, you need to be especially alert to signs of sickness in your kitten and contact your vet if you think it's ill.

~ 25 ~

~ 26 ~

~ 27 ~

~ 28 ~

July

~ 29 ~

~ 30 ~

~ 31 ~

The coats of these lilac point Siamese kittens will retain that glacial whiteness even in adulthood. Their points, hardly visible now, will eventually deepen into a subtle lilac shade, and their dark blue eyes will soon become a sapphire hue.

August

The **August** kitten is trim, demure and can be stand-offish and undemonstrative. It is also one of those ‘fussy pussies’. August kits can be finicky feeders, so its food must be tasty, nutritious and fastidiously clean. This goes for personal hygiene, too. Frenetic bouts of washing occur throughout the day so kitty can be relied on to look perfectly groomed at all times. With the accent on its dainty paws, it is a dab hand with toys that dangle at the end of wands – perfect mousing practice! The loyal August kitten is probably best kept as a much-loved single pet.

August

~ 1 ~

~ 2 ~

A small black kitten turned up on the doorstep of No 10 Downing Street, the official home of the British Prime Minister, on October 10, 1953 which, coincidentally, happened to be the day of Prime Minister Winston Churchill's famous speech to the Conservative Party at Margate in Kent. The kitten lingered, was taken in by the staff and promptly christened Margate.

~ 3 ~

~ 4 ~

~ 5 ~

Kitten Care
A kitten's playful little paw can pull over pot plants, often with dire results, so try to keep all plants out of its reach. Some house plants are poisonous to cats and these include ivy, diffenbachia, poinsettia, hyacinth and castor oil plants. Outside plants include lupin, monkshood, iris and foxglove.

~ 6 ~

~ 7 ~

August

What a lovely kitten! A red and white non-pedigree, this innocent looking little soul will grow into a fine, handsome young cat. The light of adventure can already been seen in its eyes – perhaps it's planning its next exciting escapade!

August

~ 8 ~

~ 9 ~

Kitten Names
August kittens are sincere, dependable, neat, perfectionist types, practical and 'earthy'. Names for your **August** boy kitten could be: Nimrod, Reginald, Treasure, Herby, Garden Tiger, Captain Virgo, Mister Mittens; and for your **August** girl kitten: Vesta, Virginia, Martha, Tabitha, Fussypussy or Tabitha Twitchett, Borage, Sage, Lovage, Mary or Myrtle Mittens.

~ 10 ~

~ 11 ~

~ 12 ~

~ 13 ~

~ 14 ~

Kitten Care
Mother cats feed their new-born kittens on demand. However, while still drinking her milk, the youngsters begin to need a little more substance to their meals and can be introduced to cereals and baby food. When completely weaned, four small meals a day up to eight months old is a good guide. In the very young kitten, the tummy is about the size of a walnut, so 'little and often' is the key phrase. After eight months old, your kitten will probably require larger meals around three times a day, and then at nine months, two meals will be sufficient.

August

Two different breeds: a blue Persian Longhair adult and a cream British Shorthair kitten. We perceive them as different, but to one other they're simply cats, and in the time-honoured fashion the younger snuggles close to the elder for protection and warmth.

August

~ 15 ~

~ 16 ~

~ 17 ~

CAT-NAPPERS

'Kittens are born with their eyes shut. They open them in about six days, take a look around, then close them again for the better part of their lives.'

STEPHEN BAKER.

'In my experience, kittens... and beds seem to be a natural combination.'

DR LOUIS J CAMUTI

~ 18 ~

~ 19 ~

~ 20 ~

~ 21 ~

August

This Red Persian Longhair kitten looks perfect in every way. Will its portrait find its way onto a chocolate box cover, or will it become a champion show cat? Whatever its destiny, this feline charmer would make the purrfect pet!

August

~ 22 ~

~ 23 ~

~ 24 ~

Mother Care
Mother cat recognises her kittens by their scent. If one of her babies wanders away from the nest, she will sniff at it and return it to the nest. If the kitten isn't her own she will sniff, fail to recognise its smell and leave it alone. Later, the kitten will instinctively begin to use its own sense of smell – usually on a member of its human family! This is more than just a friendly 'rubbing'. The kitten is marking that person with its facial scent glands, at the same time collecting the scent of the human on its fur.

~ 25 ~

~ 26 ~

~ 27 ~

~ 28 ~

August

~ 29 ~

~ 30 ~

~ 31 ~

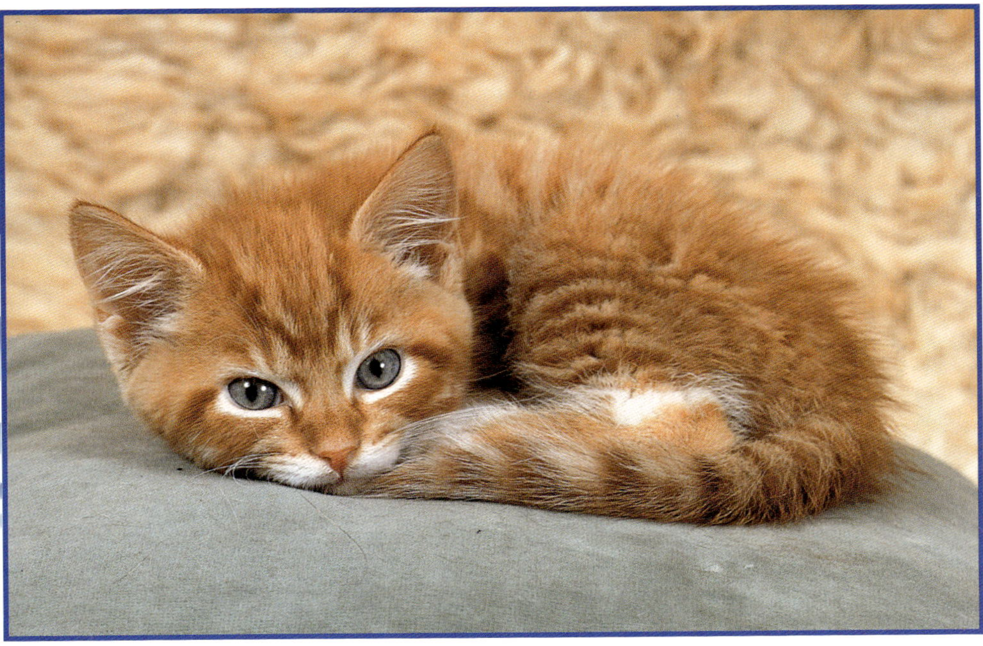

'...I rested my eyes on her graceful little body, curled up in a ball and wrapped round with her tail like a parcel... jaded spirits find natural relief in the sight of creatures whose little cups of happiness can be so easily filled to the brim.'

AGNES REPPLIER

September

The **September** kitten is an adorable kitten. Pretty, charming and at one with its environment, this kitten has impeccable taste. Amiable, pleasure-loving and a mite self-indulgent, its aim is to find a 'significant other', thereafter to enjoy a union of blissful harmony. This shapely kitty is a photographer's dream, blending with props and backgrounds with easy charm. September kit's owners are triple blessed since their pussy tunes in to their every mood, becoming confidante, comforting fur muff and a total pleasure to behold. Too good to be true? You'd better believe it. September kittens are perfect through and through!

September

~ 1 ~

~ 2 ~

~ 3 ~

~ 4 ~

~ 5 ~

~ 6 ~

~ 7 ~

Kitten Names

September kittens are charming, luxury-loving, fond of the arts, sometimes indolent and 'airy'. Names for your **September** boy kitten could be: Lord Fauntleroy, Nijinsky, Nureyev, Septimus, Sarabandit, Prince Charming; and for your **September** girl kitten: Aphrodite, Sweetness'n'light, Pretty Posy, Clementina, Helen (of Troy), Pavlova, Isadora Duncan, Deborah, Melissa or SugarsweetSu.

Kitten Care

There's a special way to hold your kitten. Do this gently but firmly, placing your left hand under its front legs, while supporting the hind-quarters with your right. Sudden noises or movements could startle your kitten, so always be aware that it may try to leap from your grasp.

September

"We've had our dinner so now we'll clean our paws – have to keep smart, just as Mum taught us!" Two little British Shorthairs get on with their toilet, as good kittens do. The third poses obediently for the camera...

September

~ 8 ~

~ 9 ~

'There's no doubt that as a pick-me-up for delicate kittens, the sea air is much to be recommended. It is quite wonderful to see the transformation in these little mites after a few days of sunshine by the seaside. Their eyes become so clear and bright ..!'
FRANCES SIMPSON (c1902)

~ 10 ~

~ 11 ~

~ 12 ~

~ 13 ~

~ 14 ~

KITTEN CARE
In the biological sense your kitten becomes an adult cat at around eight months, some even earlier and some later. From then on, two meals, one in the morning and one at night-time, is the norm. But from the outset, choose the kind of food that is convenient both for you and your kitten. Do not overfeed, otherwise your little friend will get used to only large meals. Healthy kittens, and cats, *never* get fat! Try not to fall into the trap of feeding your kitten only the food it thinks it likes best. Fussy owners often create fussy feeders!

September

~ 15 ~

~ 16 ~

~ 17 ~

Juliette de Bairacli Levy advises a new kitten-owner to give the kitten a name, immediately. 'The calling of that chosen word, its name, by its new owner is comforting. Gypsies vow it's unlucky for companion animals not to be named as soon as they're owned by a human family.'

~ 18 ~

~ 19 ~

~ 20 ~

~ 21 ~

September

~ 22 ~

~ 23 ~

On the health of young kittens, Mrs Frances Simpson (c 1902) has this to say: 'The health of kittens is in their weight; and a kitten should weigh one pound *(450 g)* to every month. So, if you find a three months old kit much below three pounds *(1.4.kg)*, you should feed him up...'

~ 24 ~

~ 25 ~

MICHAELMAS MISCHIEF
It is said that a 'Blackberry Kitten' or kitten born on Michaelmas Day, or even just after its passing, will bring much luck to its owner ~ but will also be very mischievous. If you happen to own a blackberry cat, you will be both blessed and your patience sorely tried!

~ 26 ~

~ 27 ~

~ 28 ~

September

~ 29 ~

~ 30 ~

When a new kitten or puppy is brought into the house, existing pets will see the newcomer as a challenge to their own territory, so you can expect a flurry of hisses, growls and much gnashing of sharp white teeth – just to show who's boss! But when introduced to each other at an early stage, kittens and puppies *can* and *do*, co-exist quite happily together. The puppy will grow at a much faster rate than the kitten, so it is wise to ensure that games played in comparative safety earlier on are not now too boisterous for your little kitten!

October

The **October** kitten can be a little demon. Set to become a haunter of back alleys, with a penchant for dustbins and their decaying contents, this kit gets into the mood quite early. From the outset, it holds its own counsel, and one look into those glittering, hypnotic eyes tells you that this is an 'old soul'. However, October kitten can be possessive and loyal towards its person. But, put a foot, or hand, wrong and an enemy is made for life. With deeply secretive natures, these kits are the embryonic 'witch cat' they tend to become in later life.

October

~ 1 ~

~ 2 ~

Writer and naturalist Henry David Thoreau describes the kitten's amazing physique: 'A kitten is so flexible that she is almost double; the hind parts are equivalent to another kitten with which the forepart plays. She does not discover that her tail belongs to her until you tread on it.'

~ 3 ~

~ 4 ~

Poetry in Motion
Cats walk on their toes, not on the soles of their feet. They are agile and display an unusual grace, even when they're young. As they leap into the air, their movements are smooth like an accomplished ballerina. A joy to behold, kittens are never guilty of an ungraceful move.

~ 5 ~

~ 6 ~

~ 7 ~

October

"How did I get up here? More to the point, how do I get down?" Sometimes, kittens can be too adventurous for their own good and have to be carefully lifted to safety! Awkward places often attract brave young kits.

October

October

These young Burmese show the breed's three main coat colours: brown, blue and chocolate. Burmese have been a firm favourite for many years and are known for their intelligence and friendliness.

October

~ 8 ~

STAR-FATED
It is said that it's possible to know yourself through your cat. Certainly, many of us would like to equate ourselves with a small, pretty and playful kitten! Kittens, too, are sensitive little creatures, and while a charming attribute in the feline, is guilelessly 'sensitive' something we truly yearn to be?
It's possible, however, by astrological means to assess your kitten's character and principle motivations, and of course your own, to decide upon your suitability as pet and owner. After all, your kitten-cat could be around for perhaps 15 years or more, so it's worth finding out your compatibility ratings!

~ 9 ~

~ 10 ~

~ 11 ~

~ 12 ~

~ 13 ~

~ 14 ~

October

~ 15 ~

Kitten Names

October kittens are deep, secretive, jealously possessive, witch-like and 'watery'. Names for your **October** boy kitten could be: Pyewacket, Nick, Caliban, Merlin, Maigret, Octavius, Eliphas Levi, Black Jack, Princeofpentacles, Shadow, Spookyboots; and your **October** girl kitten: Hecate, Lilith, Persephone, Tarot, Octavia, Henbane, Clawz'n'pawz or Morgana le Fey, Nocturne or Shady.

~ 16 ~

~ 17 ~

Kitten Care

Kittens are, by nature, lively, boisterous and mischievous. Sometimes when the family is at home or when elderly people are around, playful pussy may get under their feet, possibly causing a serious accident, not only to the human concerned but also to itself. At times like these, why not allow your kitten to play quietly by itself with its toys in a kitten-pen? The kitten's playfulness can often lead it into trouble, and the wise owner will act quickly to avoid problems. Beware dangling tablecloth edges and, whenever necessary, gently unhook your kitten's claws from curtains and heavy 'flocked' wallpaper.

~ 18 ~

~ 19 ~

~ 20 ~

~ 21 ~

October

~ 22 ~

~ 23 ~

'A small, peach coloured teddy bear was Alexander's particular friend. He'd throw it into the air and hug it with impassioned delight. Then, shaking it in his mouth and uttering throaty, possessive growls, he'd fall fast asleep, as kittens do, his arm curved lovingly around Teddy's neck.'
JOAN MOORE

~ 24 ~

~ 25 ~

~ 26 ~

~ 27 ~

~ 28 ~

October

Founding Felines
The first Siamese cats introduced to the West had dark seal brown coloured points and the all-white kittens produced by the seal-point queens at the time were considered by Victorian breeders to be poor examples of the breed. As such, many early foundation stock Siamese kittens were ill-advisedly destroyed.

~ 29 ~

~ 30 ~

~ 31 ~

Somali kittens make the ideal pet – they're lively, inquisitive and intelligent. They hold chirruping converations with their owners and can get into the most hair-raising scrapes. As they reach adulthood, they retain these youthful ways to become playful, stimulating companions.

November

The **November** kitten is a reckless little bundle of energy! Charm and a sort of clumsy optimism are endearing features of this little clown-cat whose fiery spirit you must never be tempted to dowse. Deeply upset if its adventuring ways are curtailed, just try to be vigilant and ensure this 'free spirit' doesn't wander too far. A lover of sport, especially of hunting, November kitten makes an excellent mouser – mainly for the game of catching its prey, not eating it! This happy, chirruping youngster will grow into a happy chirruping adult – complete with the same prankish ways it always had.

November

~ 1 ~

~ 2 ~

Kitten Names

November kittens are free spirits, adventurous, recklessly optimistic, enjoy sporting activities and are 'fiery'. Names for your **November** boy kitten could be: Cernunnos, Happyhunter, Domino, Backgammon, Dicey, Forest Ranger, Bravo, Jester, Lucky; and for your **November** girl kitten: Diana, Boudicca, Amazongirl, Sparky, Little Chancer, Roma, Gypsy Girl or Romany Princess.

~ 3 ~

~ 4 ~

~ 5 ~

~ 6 ~

'...Dinah washed her children's faces: first she held the poor thing down by its ears with one paw, then with the other she rubbed its face all over...she was hard at work on the white kitten, which was lying quite still and trying to purr...'

Lewis Carroll

~ 7 ~

November

Young kittens love to explore. This one treads carefully, half expecting some huge predator to appear. It's an exciting new world of big green forests with wild exciting smells. To a very small kitten, a garden is a magical place!

November

~ 8 ~

~ 9 ~

~ 10 ~

~ 11 ~

~ 12 ~

~ 13 ~

~ 14 ~

Kitten Care

Is your kitchen a warm and friendly place where food can be found? Then it's probably your kitten's favourite playground. It can also be one of the most dangerous areas in the house. Most household cleaning products are toxic to felines as also are paints, sprays and solvents which can be absorbed through the skin or paw pads. Cookers and hotplates can burn delicate paws, and holes in skirting boards, openings in the back of washing machines and refrigerators and small spaces behind cupboards and storage heaters are all potentially dangerous should the kitten become trapped and its absence remain unnoticed.

November

~ 15 ~

~ 16 ~

Show Potential
In some pedigree breeds, it is difficult to assess a kitten's show potential since adult configuration and colouration does not fully develop until early maturity. However, don't be deterred from showing your kitten in its own breed and 'special' classes – same-breed kittens competing against each other stand an equal chance!

~ 17 ~

~ 18 ~

'He loved books and when he found one open on the table he would lie down on it, turn over the edges of the leaves with his paw and, after a while, fall fast asleep, for all the world as if he had been reading a fashionable novel.'
Theophile Gautier

~ 19 ~

~ 20 ~

~ 21 ~

November

~ 22 ~

~ 23 ~

'A good guide to the health of kittens is their weight; a kitten to be in really prime condition should weigh one pound to every month, say up to six months old. If you find a three-month-old kit much below three pounds, you should feed him up.'

FRANCES SIMPSON (c1902)

~ 24 ~

~ 25 ~

~ 26 ~

'If kittens are attacked with distemper and the weather is warm and fine, put them out on the lawn in the sunshine. Fresh air works wonders for diseased animals. In the case of sickness, soda and milk is sometimes the only food that can be kept down.

FRANCES SIMPSON (c1902)

~ 27 ~

~ 28 ~

November

~ 29 ~

~ 30 ~

It's fun when you have a littermate to share your adventures. These two kittens stay close to keep each other company. But what about lunch first? There's nothing like a good meal to make a kitten feel brave and fearless!

December

The **December** kitten is careful, cautious and always in control. Even from a very young age, this dignified young December kit projects an air of authority ,which is quite impressive in one of such tender years. These feline folk are kindly and enduringly patient with their more frisky siblings, but one withering look can quell the most unrepentant creature into total submission. Lacking the skittishness of other kittens, the December youngster is solemn and old beyond its years. The popular saying that 'you can't put an old head on young shoulders' just isn't true in this wise little kitty's case!

December

~ 1 ~

~ 2 ~

~ 3 ~

~ 4 ~

~ 5 ~

~ 6 ~

~ 7 ~

Ever-loving

Kittens purr loudly when stroked and petted and it doesn't take them long to learn that weaving themselves affectionately round their owners legs is often rewarded by a bout of petting. Responding readily to human affection is probably one of the main reasons why we love our kittens so much...

'A kitten may be considered a cat when it has shed its very first teeth. This process takes place between six and nine months – and often during this period, pussy cat is out of sorts and will refuse her food, for the gums are tender and sore.'

Frances Simpson (c 1902)

December

This lovely little cream kitten is a non-pedigree. Sometimes a rescued or an abandoned kitten can make a really good pet. They are generally healthy and when neutered or spayed will not be tempted to wander, making instead delightful companions.

December

~ 8 ~

~ 9 ~

Kitten Names
December kittens are carefully cautious, dignified, 'in control', authoritarian, figures of power and 'earthy'. Names for your **December** boy kitten could be: Moses, Abacus, Uriah, Everest, President, Guru, Prince, Marquis, Sultan, Mighty Mog; and your **December** girl kitten: Prudence Kitten, Patience, Holly, Poppy, Pansy, Lady, Queenie, Crown Princess or Elizabeth.

~ 10 ~

~ 11 ~

~ 12 ~

~ 13 ~

~ 14 ~

Kitten Care
The basic requirements and necessities for a happy healthy kitten include food, warmth, security and a loving, caring relationship with its owner. Always ensure a comfortable, draughtproof box to sleep in, food and water for when the kitten is hungry or thirsty and a clean litter tray within easy reach.

Have lots of fun playing with your new kitten! Happy times together will not only strengthen the bond between you, it will also help your kitten adjust to its new home and family. Treated sensibly and with kindness, your little friend will respond with a lifetime of affection and loyalty.

December

Sweet little Somalis make truly appealing pets. They are playful with a quiet voice and gentle manner. They are easy to groom since their hair tends not to mat. Somalis are active and need space in which to play.

December

~ 15 ~

~ 16 ~

~ 17 ~

An Irish proverb vows: 'The three merriest things in the world are a cat's kitten, a goat's kid and a young widow.' And Beryl Swift proclaims: 'When kittens nap in pansy beds and drowse the sunny hours, I can't tell which are spotted cats and which are spotted flowers!'

~ 18 ~

~ 19 ~

~ 20 ~

~ 21 ~

December

Birmans, sometimes called the Sacred Cat of Burma, are a fascinating breed. This kitten will grow into a majestic looking cat with snowy white paws and typical face mask similar to the Siamese, which also comes from South East Asia.

December

~ 22 ~

~ 23 ~

~ 24 ~

~ 25 ~

~ 26 ~

~ 27 ~

~ 28 ~

Feline Fantasies

What does a kitten dream of? We shall never know, but since that special feline magic has been an endless source of inspiration to all those who've known and loved one, perhaps we could venture a guess. 'Bright, nodding flowers; gay butterflies? Sweet scented grass; blue Summer skies?' Or, 'Cool woodland path; dancing leaves and sunlight glinting thru tall trees? A puff of down, gently touched by paw, to float up and away 'til seen no more?' Who knows what kittens dream of?. Their sleeping thoughts are gossamer things; known only to themselves; fey, enchanting and tantalisingly, secret...

December

~ 29 ~

~ 30 ~

~ 31 ~

Burmillas are the fascinating result of an original mating between a Lilac Burmese and a Silver Chinchilla Longhair. These kittens will have the friendly, companionable characteristics of the Burmese and the exotic beauty of the Chinchilla – including those magnificent eyes!

Acknowledgements

Pages 43, 60 and 81: Quotes by Juliette de Bairacli Levy are from *Cats – Naturally*, published by Faber & Faber Ltd.